GA
CENGAGE Learning

Novels for Students, Volume 35

Project Editor: Sara Constantakis Rights Acquisition and Management: Margaret Chamberlain-Gaston, Leitha Etheridge-Sims, Kelly Quin, Aja Perales Composition: Evi Abou-El-Seoud Manufacturing: Drew Kalasky

Imaging: John Watkins

Product Design: Pamela A. E. Galbreath, Jennifer Wahi Content Conversion: Katrina Coach Product Manager: Meggin Condino © 2011 Gale, Cengage Learning ALL RIGHTS RESERVED. No part of this work covered by the copyright herein may be reproduced, transmitted, stored, or used in any form or by any means graphic, electronic, or mechanical, including but not limited to photocopying, recording, scanning, digitizing, taping, Web distribution, information networks, or information storage and retrieval systems, except as permitted under Section 107 or 108 of the 1976 United States Copyright Act, without the prior written permission

For product information and technology assistance, contact us at **Gale Customer Support, 1-800-877-4253.**
For permission to use material from this text or product, submit all requests online at **www.cengage.com/permissions**.
Further permissions questions can be emailed to **permissionrequest@cengage.com**   While every effort has been made to ensure the reliability of the information presented in this publication, Gale, a part of Cengage Learning, does not guarantee the accuracy of the data contained herein. Gale accepts no payment for listing; and inclusion in the publication of any organization, agency, institution, publication, service, or individual does not imply endorsement of the editors or publisher. Errors brought to the attention of the publisher and verified to the satisfaction of the publisher will be corrected in future editions.

Gale
27500 Drake Rd.
Farmington Hills, MI, 48331-3535

ISBN-13: 978-1-4144-6698-9
ISBN-10: 1-4144-6698-6
ISSN 1094-3552

This title is also available as an e-book.
ISBN-13: 978-1-4144-7364-2

ISBN-10: 1-4144-7364-8
Contact your Gale, a part of Cengage Learning sales
representative for ordering information.

Printed in the United States of America
1 2 3 4 5 6 7 14 13 12 11 10

Wicked: The Life and Times of the Wicked Witch of the West

Gregory Maguire 1995

Introduction

Wicked: The Life and Times of the Wicked Witch of the West is the first adult novel that Gregory Maguire published after a distinguished early career writing fiction for children. It should be stressed that this novel covers adult themes and includes descriptions of adult sexual experiences, as well as significant violence, and is not recommended for younger readers.

In *Wicked*, Maguire explores the back story of two characters from L. Frank Baum's fictional land of Oz: the Wicked Witch of the East and the Wicked Witch of the West. Were they really wicked? And if so, what made them that way? He tells the story of Elphaba, the Wicked Witch of the West, who is born mysteriously green, very smart, somewhat prickly, and with a deep devotion to equal justice for all creatures in a world ruled by despots. He also tells the story of Galinda, who later changes her name to Glinda, who begins life as a spoiled and vain socialite and becomes a powerful sorceress. Whether Glinda is a "good" witch or not is ambiguous, although she is clearly not as tormented as either Elphaba, the Wicked Witch of the West, or her sister Nessarose, the Wicked Witch of the East. Neither sister sets out to become wicked, in fact, both sisters consider themselves to be working for the good, Elphaba by resisting the oppression of the Animals, and Nessarose by enforcing her vision of the virtuous Unionist religion on Munchkinland. One of Maguire's central themes in the book is the ways in which a quest for virtue and justice can itself warp the seeker, leading him or her down paths that are as destructive as those against which they rebel.

Author Biography

Maguire was born on June 9, 1954, in Albany, New York. His mother, Helen, died giving birth to him. He and his three older siblings were split up among relatives, and for a short time, the baby was placed in an orphanage. His father, John, a newspaper reporter, eventually married Marie Mc Auliff, a poet, and reunited the family, adding a couple more siblings along the way. Maguire's history with the *Wizard of Oz* has its roots in his childhood. After seeing the movie on television, Maguire led a group of siblings and neighborhood children in a performance but expanded the cast to include Tinker Bell, Captain Hook, and Peter Pan. In an interview with Bev Goldberg on the American Library Association's Web log *AL Inside Scoop*, he recalled that he told the other children "we need to have more than one bad guy so we can see who is worse." That particular game was interrupted when his stepmother discovered in the nick of time that Maguire's thirteen-month old brother was suffocating in a hiding place under the porch. The baby was fine, but an imagination was fired. Maguire produced several hundred manuscripts between the ages of eight and eighteen, but as he told *Book selling This Week*, he "was hopelessly fecund but not talented enough to be considered a wunderkind." He completed his bachelor's degree at the State University of New York at Albany and his doctorate in English and American studies at Tufts

University. While he was a student, he wrote a children's book titled *The Lightning Time*, which was published when he was twenty three.

He taught and codirected the Simmons College Center for the Study of Children's Literature and founded Children's Literature New England in 1985. Although he had been publishing children's books all along, it was while living in England in the 1990s that he suffered a bout of what he called, in the *Bookselling This Week* article, "financial embarrassment." Maguire wrote: "I began to be worried about being able to pay my bills.... I could see the time was growing ripe and that if I didn't do it, somebody else was going to have that very good idea and do it." *Wicked* was Maguire's first novel for adults, and its success freed him from teaching and allowed him to write full time. He has continued to write books for children and for adults ever since. In 2003, the Broadway musical *Wicked* debuted; it is based on an adaptation of Maguire's best-selling novel, and it has broken box-office records around the world.

In 2004, after same-sex marriage was legalized in Massachusetts, Maguire married Andy Newman, a painter. Together, they have adopted three children, Luke and Alex from Cambodia and Helen from Guatemala. In 2005, when asked by Bob Minzes heimer of *USA Today* about the intersection of the popular and the subversive in his life, Maguire said, I'm a father of three young kids, a practicing Catholic, a registered voter who does vote, a taxpayer, a volunteer on the boards of local charities.... Yet I am also an openly gay married man, a critic of the current administration, an occasional public dissenter about Vatican policy and practices.... so 'subversive' is perhaps more flattering than accurate.

Prologue: On the Yellow Brick Road

The Witch descends out of the sky above Oz, where she eavesdrops on four travelers, a Lion, a Scarecrow, a Tin Woodman and a little girl, who gossip about the witch's true nature. As the group runs for shelter from the gathering storm, the Witch recognizes Dorothy's shoes and vows to retrieve them. When the rain begins, the Witch hides herself in the roots of a large tree, since water of any kind burns her like fire.

Part I: Munchkinlanders

THE ROOT OF EVIL

Frex, a Unionist minister, prepares for a crucial sermon as his wife, Melena, prepares to give birth to their first child. They spar affectionately over whose task is more momentous before Frex leaves for Rush Margins, the nearby town.

THE CLOCK OF THE TIME DRAGON

Frex stops in a neighbor's house to find a woman to help Melena with childbirth. Melena is unpopular because she was born wealthy, but the neighbor promises to send someone. Frex prepares to preach against the faith which is in opposition to his Unionist beliefs.

THE BIRTH OF A WITCH

Frex arrives in Rush Margins just before the Clock of the Time Dragon, an enormous mechanical dragon whose side opens to reveal a puppet show. As Frex preaches, the Dragon's puppets show a story of a preacher like Frex, with an unfaithful wife like Melena. As the puppet preacher is run through with a pike and roasted, one of Frex's parishioners attacks him. An old woman hides him in her storeroom. The crones who help Melena through childbirth hide her in the Dragon itself. When the baby is born, she is bright green, and they cannot determine her sex. The crones debate killing the green baby, and she bites the finger off one with her razor sharp teeth. They leave the baby and her unconscious mother inside the dragon and run away.

MALADIES AND REMEDIES

Melena's nanny arrives to help with the green baby, who is named Elphaba. Nanny quizzes both parents about what could have caused Elphaba's color, but she cannot find an answer. Frex believes it is an evil spirit, but Melena confesses that she might have slept with passing strangers while Frex was away. Nanny tries several unsuccessful folk remedies, and when she is convinced she cannot fix the situation, she returns home.

Media Adaptations

- An unabridged audiobook of *Wicked* was recorded in 2005 and is available from Harper Audio.

- In May 2003, the Broadway musical version of *Wicked* opened at the Gershwin Theater in New York City. The music and lyrics were written by Stephen Schwartz, and Winnie Holtzman wrote the "book," or text, of the musical. It starred Idina Menzel as Elphaba, Kristin Chenoweth as Glinda, and Joel Gray as the Wizard. Menzel won the 2004 Tony Award for Best Actress, and the show has gone on to break box-office records in New York, Los Angeles, Chicago, and many cities around the world. Although there is no video of the production, the original cast recording is available from Decca Broadway on CD or as a download.

- Although it is not an adaptation of *Wicked* but rather the other way around, the 1939 movie musical *The Wizard of Oz* is a predecessor to *Wicked*. A holiday staple on television, the movie, starring Judy Garland, Billie Burke, Ray Bolger, and Jack Haley, with Margaret Hamilton as the Wicked Witch of the West, is available on DVD from Warner Home Video.

THE QUADLING GLASSBLOWER

Melena and Elphaba are in the yard when they are surprised by a stranger, a Quadling glassblower named Turtle Heart. Melena feeds him, and he plays with baby Elphaba before blowing her a glass disk in which the future can be seen. He sees Frex and Nanny approaching, but he says they will not arrive until evening, so Melena takes the stranger to bed for the afternoon while Elphaba plays with the glass disk.

GEOGRAPHIES OF THE SEEN AND UNSEEN

Frex returns home with Nanny and is charmed by their new visitor. He explains the geography of Oz to Turtle Heart, who has never left Quadling country, and attempts to explain how the religious views of the Unionists are endangered by the pleasure religion. At dinner, Nanny adds the history of those who believe in Lurline, the Fairy Queen whose daughters, the Ozmas, have ruled for centuries. Frex objects to this talk of Lurline, while Melena reminisces about meeting the current Ozma as a young debutante.

CHILD'S PLAY

Nanny declares that Elphaba must have other children to play with. Melena objects, but Nanny threatens to tell Frex that Melena and Turtle Heart have been having a secret affair. They take the girl to Gawnette's home, where Elphaba joins a pack of grubby neighborhood children.

DARKNESS ABROAD

When Frex says that his mission is to the downtrodden, Turtle Heart says that the Quadlings are downtrodden, and he tells them of the ruby miners who have disrupted the delicate ecosystem of his country. Elphaba speaks her first word, "horrors," and Melena, trying to dissuade Frex from dragging her into the Quadling swamps, confesses that she is pregnant. Later, Elphaba disappears, and after a frantic search, during which Turtle Heart collapses, they find her in the arms of a terrible beast, repeating her first word.

Part II: Gillikin

GALINDA

Galinda, a vain and beautiful Gillikinese girl, meets Dr. Dillamond, a Goat who is a lecturer at her college, on the train into Shiz. Madame Morrible, the headmistress of the college, pairs her with Elphaba as a roommate. Galinda and Elphaba are very different, and they do not really like one another. The Wizard proclaims a ban on all Animal mobility, both in transportation and in the professions. Dr. Dillamond is deeply upset, and Elphaba takes on his cause. Madame Morrible suggests that Galinda take up sorcery as her academic specialty and hints that if she does so, perhaps Galinda can be freed from her roommate.

BOQ

Boq, a childhood friend of Elphaba's and now a fellow student, climbs a tree to get a better look at the girls' dormitory windows and is caught by Elphaba. Boq admits to having a crush on Galinda, and Elphaba says she will arrange a meeting. When Galinda explains that she cannot return his feelings because he is from a different ethnic group and social class, Boq proposes that they all become friends. Galinda cannot see the point in that. Boq has a chance encounter with Elphaba, who is working for Dr. Dillamond, whom Boq admires, and they become friends over a shared interest in his research. When Elphaba explains that Dr. Dillamond's research is hampered by the inadequate library, Boq offers to use his library to help. Crope and Tibbett join the research efforts, and once a week they all meet at the cafe´. When Elphaba receives an invitation from Galinda to join her and the other rich girls at a lake cottage, Boq insists she accept. When they arrive, they learn it is a cruel joke. Back in Shiz, Dr. Dillamond is murdered.

THE CHARMED CIRCLE

Dr. Dillamond's murder is covered up, and Ama Clutch succumbs to the very disorder that Galinda lied to Madam Morrible about earlier, and she now speaks only to inanimate objects. Galinda changes her name to Glinda, the name Dr. Dillamond called her on the train. Elphaba sends for Nanny and Nessarose. Boq meets Nessarose and Nanny at the coach and is amazed by Nessarose's beauty, despite her handicap of having no arms. Glinda is both awed by Nessarose's strange beauty and annoyed by her demanding neediness and overbearing religious fervor. In a lecture, Dr. Dillamond's successor, Dr. Nikidik, uncorks a bottle of "Extract of Biologic Intention" which accidentally animates a set of stag's horns, nearly killing a new student, the prince Fiyero from Vinkus, who enters the room late. The Thropp sisters are summoned, with Nanny, to Madame Morrible's chambers, where she delivers a pair of miraculous shoes, covered in glass beads that shimmer and pulse, that their father has made for Nessarose. There is no gift for Elphaba.

When Ama Clutch is about to die, Glinda uses all her skills to cast a spell that brings the old woman back to sanity. She tells them that it was the Grommetik that killed Dr. Dillamond. After a stingy funeral, Madame Morrible calls the girls into her office, casts a binding spell on them, and tells them that in return for great power, she can make them Adepts and give them each a section of Oz to rule over. In return, they will have to feed her information that will help keep the Wizard in power. When Glinda and Nessarose try to discuss it afterwards, both girls faint. Later, Avaric proposes they visit the Philosophy Club, a notorious sex club. Elphaba prevents Glinda from going along, while Nanny escorts Nessarose home. Boq, Avaric, Tibbett, Fiyero, Shenshen, and Pfannee all go to the Philosophy Club, which is run by the crone Yackle and the dwarf from the Clock of the Time Dragon. There is a disturbing incident involving a Tiger, from which Tibbett never quite recovers. Elphaba tells Glinda that they need to go to the Emerald City and meet with the Wizard. It takes them nearly a week to get there. After waiting five days, the girls get an audience with the Wizard, who appears as a dancing, luminescent skeleton. When Elphaba presents Dr. Dillamond's evidence—in full faith that if the Wizard only knew the situation, he would reverse his restrictions on Animals—he mocks her and tells her that morality has nothing to do with his decisions. Elphaba replies that if she believed that, she would be obligated to try to kill him. The Wizard accuses them of being pawns in a game they do not understand, and he vanishes. Elphaba tells Glinda she is not going back to Shiz and melts into the crowd.

Part III: City of Emeralds

Five years later, Fiyero encounters Elphaba, but she denies her identity. He tracks her to an abandoned building, forces his way in, and demands that she tell him why she disappeared. She finally admits that she has gone underground and is working to overthrow the Wizard. She tells him he must leave and never come back, that it is too dangerous to be seen with her. Fiyero is surprised by the strength of his attraction to her and vows to come back. She allows him to return, and they begin a deep and passionate love affair. They argue about Elphaba's political work. One day, Fiyero witnesses an act of unspeakable brutality against a family of Bears. Elphaba tells him she needs two weeks of solitude to prepare for what is to come. He objects, fearing she is using it as an excuse to disappear. During this break, Fiyero encounters Glinda and Crope. Glinda is glamorous and married to a rich man. She tells Fiyero that Nessarose is in town with the Eminent Thropp and that she hates Elphaba for abandoning her. When the two-week break is over, Fiyero is relieved to find Elphaba in her apartment. She warns him not to be in any crowded places on Lurlinemas Eve, and they argue once more about the effectiveness of violence. On Lurlinemas Eve, Fiyero stalks her through the town, watching as she waits in the square outside a theater. Her target is Madame Morrible. Just as Elphaba is about to spring, Madame Morrible is engulfed in a crowd of small children. Fiyero watches Elphaba struggle, then fail in her quest to kill Madame Morrible. He goes back to her apartment, where he is beaten into unconsciousness.

Elphaba seeks refuge in the mauntery, or convent, of Saint Glinda. There is blood on her wrists, but she seems unharmed.

Part IV: In the Vinkus

THE VOYAGE OUT

Seven years later, Sister Saint Aelphaba is released from the mauntery into the care of Oatsie Manglehand, a woman drover who is leading a caravan into the Vinkus country. The Mother Superior pays her to take Elphaba and a small boy. Elphaba is silent. She reflects on her life in the mauntery and how it was Tibbett, brought into her infirmary for the dying, who teased her back into herself again. Elphaba and a boy, Liir, befriend the cook's dog, Killyjoy. Elphaba invites a swarm of bees to come along, much to the alarm of the other travelers. As they climb the Kumbrica pass, the cook disappears one night. The caravan emerges from the pass, and a Yunamata messenger arrives to say that the body of the cook has been found at the bottom of a cliff, covered in lesions. The other travelers begin to call Elphaba a witch, and they claim that it was her bees that killed the cook. The group encounters the Scow tribe, led by the massive and elderly Princess Nastoya. Elphaba is summoned to the Scow temple, where the princess reveals herself to be an enchanted Elephant. She tells Elphaba that she must be careful and gives Elphaba three crows. As they approach Kiamo Ko, Elphaba rescues an infant monkey from the jaws of Killyjoy.

At Kiamo Ko, Liir says he is staying with her, and although Elphaba still seems not to recognize him, the narrator states that Liir was coming into the house of his father.

THE JASPER GATES OF KIAMO KO

Elphaba arrives at Kiamo Ko determined to confess to Fiyero's widow Sarima that she had had an affair with Fiyero. Elphaba intends to head into the wilderness after that and become a hermit, but her plans are foiled when Sarima refuses to hear her confession. "This is my house and I choose to hear what I want," she tells Elphaba. She puts Elphaba and Liir up in the southeast tower. Fiyero's children take to tormenting Liir, who is slow and fat. Elphaba asks the sisters what happened to Fiyero, and they tell her that Sarima believes he was having an affair with Glinda and that Sir Chuffery had him killed, but they think it was for political reasons, as his body has never been found. Elphaba finds an enchanted Grimmerie, or encyclopedia of magic. Sarima tells her it was left at Kiamo Ko by an old wizard, who said it was from another world and needed a safe hiding place. Manek plays a prank on Liir, hiding him in the fishwell, and then forgets about him in the excitement of Nanny's arrival. She had tracked Elphaba down via Crope, who told her that Elphaba nursed Tibbett. Two days later, they find Liir in the fish well, and Elphaba must give the boy mouth-to-mouth resuscitation. Sarima explains to Elphaba the Arjiki theory that men require hot anger to survive, while women must cultivate the cold anger of grudges and unforgiveness. While contemplating this, Elphaba gazes on a thick icicle, which then falls from the parapet and kills Manek in the courtyard below.

UPRISINGS

Nanny tells Elphaba that Nessarose has become the Eminent Thropp and Glinda, on a visit, has enchanted Nessarose's shoes to allow her to stand on her own two feet. Shell has become a secret agent in the Munchkinl and independence movement. Liir, upon being saved from the fish well, says that the golden carp told him he is Fiyero's son, an assertion that Sarima rejects. Nanny asks Elphaba whether Liir is her son, and she says she cannot know, since she spent the first year at the maunt in a deep sleep and the second year recovering. She does not remember giving birth, nor does she have any maternal feelings toward the boy, but when she left they insisted she take him along. Manek's death is a terrible blow to the family, as he was the only one who showed promise for recovering the position they lost when Fiyero died. Nor encounters a group of soldiers from the Emerald City and invites them into the castle to stay. When Nor borrows Elphaba's broom to clean the soldier's quarters, she discovers that it can fly. Elphaba learns how to fly the broom, and after receiving a letter from her father announcing that Munchkinl and has seceded from Oz and that Nessarose has declared herself the leader, she decides to travel home to see them. She has a tender reunion with her father and finds Nessarose as self-centered as always. Elphaba refuses both her father's and Nessarose's entreaties to stay and help rule Munchkinland. She returns to Kiamo Ko, only to find that Sarima and her family have been captured and Nanny is alone in the empty castle. Liir was spared, but he seems to have followed the soldiers.

Part V: The Murder and Its Afterlife

A tornado rips through Munchkinland, killing many before dropping Dorothy and her house on Nessarose. Elphaba flies home when she gets the news and finds her father brokenhearted. Glinda tells Elphaba the details, including that she gave Dorothy Nessarose's shoes and sent her to the Emerald City. Elphaba is furious, because Nessarose had promised the shoes to her. After Nessa's funeral, the Wizard summons Elphaba to an audience, where he demands to know whether she will be the next Eminent Thropp. He wants the Grimmerie; he claims that he came to Oz in search of it many years ago. Elphaba demands news of Fiyero's family and is horrified to discover that they have been murdered, except for Nor, whom the Wizard displays to her, mad and in chains. She attempts to trade the book for Nor, but the Wizard refuses. While looking for Dorothy, Elphaba encounters Boq, who is alarmed by her fury and tells her that Dorothy is just a child, not an agent of the Wizard. Elphaba is beside herself with anger at the brutality of the Wizard's regime and at her old friends' collusion. She flies to Shiz to kill Madame Morrible but arrives five minutes too late. Late at night in the park, she encounters the dwarf with the Clock of the Time Dragon. The dwarf shows her a puppet show that indicates the Wizard is her biological father, but Elphaba laughs it off. Agitated, she flies home to Kiamo Ko, where she ceases sleeping. When Dorothy and her friends approach, she becomes convinced that the Scarecrow is Fiyero in disguise. She sends the dogs to greet them and bring them to the castle, but the Tin Woodman kills them all. She sends the crows to pull the mask off the Scarecrow, but he frightens them away. She sends the bees to sting Dorothy to death, but the Scarecrow unstuffs himself to save the others. Finally, she sends the winged monkeys to bring Dorothy and the Lion to the castle. She locks Dorothy into the tower to interrogate her. Dorothy confesses that all she wants is forgiveness. Elphaba accidentally catches her dress on fire. Dorothy, seeking to save her, throws a bucket of water on her. In death, Elphaba discovers that she does indeed have a soul. Dorothy returns to the Emerald City bearing the old bottle of magical elixir. When the Wizard sees it, he flees in his balloon. No one ever sees Dorothy or the magic shoes again.

Characters

Avaric

Avaric is a handsome and wealthy Gillikinese school mate of Elphaba and Galinda, who is responsible for taking everyone to the Philosophy Club. After the death of Madame Morrible, Elphaba has a chance encounter with Avaric, who invites her to dinner. When his jaded friends take the news of Madame Morrible's death as a joke, Elphaba's agitation and despair is multiplied.

Bfee

Bfee is Boq's father and the mayor of Rush Margins.

Boq

Boq is a childhood playmate of Elphaba's whom she befriends while at university in Shiz. He falls in love with Galinda, who does not return his feelings. Boq and Elphaba become friends over a shared interest in Dr. Dillamond's work. After the death of Nessarose, Elphaba encounters Boq while trailing Dorothy. He tells her that Dorothy is just a child and tries to talk Elphaba out of her increasing paranoia, but his efforts only enrage her. She takes his defense as further evidence that Boq, like everyone else, has sold out and accepted the despotism of Oz.

Brr, the Lion

First introduced as a terrified cub upon whom Dr. Nikidik intends to experiment, Brr grows up to become the Cowardly Lion, Dorothy's companion.

Chistery

Chistery is a snow monkey that Elphaba rescues as an infant. Trying to prove Dr. Dillamond's theories, Elphaba teaches him to speak several words, although he never progresses beyond mere mimicry. Later, she surgically implants wings on him, making him her chief flying monkey.

Nick Chopper, Tin Woodman

Nick Chopper is an actual woodman upon whom Nessarose places a spell in return for the freedom of three Animals. The enchanted axe eventually chops off all his limbs and his head, but an enterprising tinsmith makes him replacement parts. He becomes one of Dorothy's companions.

Sir Chuffery

Sir Chuffery is Glinda's stupendously wealthy husband.

Ama Clutch

Ama Clutch is Galinda's chaperone. Her absence the first day of school leads to Galinda being paired with Elphaba as a roommate. After witnessing the murder of Dr. Dillamond, Ama is enchanted by Madame Morrible and then dies.

Crope

Crope is one half of a pair of "inverts," or gay students, who are part of Elphaba's circle at university. Crope eventually informs Nanny that it was Elphaba who nursed Tibbett at the end, thereby leading to Elphaba being discovered after many years' absence.

Dr. Dillamond

Dr. Dillamond is a professor at Shiz. He is a Goat and an advocate for Animal rights. Elphaba becomes his laboratory assistant, and it is through this work that she becomes determined to prove that there is no fundamental difference between humans and Animals. He is murdered by Madame Morrible's Grommetik, after which Elphaba disappears into the radical Animal rights underground.

Dwarf of the Clock of the Time Dragon

An immortal sent to Oz to keep watch over the Grimmerie, the Dwarf originally appears with the Clock of the Time Dragon the night Elphaba is born. Later, he seems to be running the Philosophy Club, and he orchestrates events the night of Tibbett's trauma. The dwarf reappears with the Clock of the Time Dragon after Madame Morrible's death, when he tells Elphaba about Yackle and that the Wizard is probably her biological father.

Fiyero

Heir to the Arjiki throne, Fiyero first appears in Dr. Nikidik's lecture, where he is nearly killed by a pair of enchanted stag's horns. He is a Vinkus prince, has blue diamonds tattooed down his face and chest, has been betrothed since childhood, and seems quite exotic to the students at Shiz.

Five years after Elphaba disappears, it is Fiyero who finds her, and they fall deeply in love before he is killed by the Gale Forces. Fiyero is probably Liir's father.

Frex

Frex is a Unionist minister married to Melena, Elphaba's mother. A religious fundamentalist, Frex is determined to win the Munchkinlanders over to Unionism from the dangers of the pleasure faith that the Clock of the Time Dragon represents. He makes the beautiful shoes for Nessarose, shoes that Elphaba sees as proof that her father loves Nessa more than he has ever loved her. Frex knows that Turtle Heart is probably the biological father of Nessarose, but because he too loved Turtle Heart deeply, he sees it as an eternal bond between them all. A kind if ineffectual man, he is loved deeply by all his children, despite his failings.

Frexspar

See Frex

Dorothy Gale

Dorothy, the heroine of *The Wizard of Oz*, is blown into Oz on the tornado that kills Nessarose. She is only a child, and she becomes a pawn of Glinda and the Wizard. Although she has been sent to kill Elphaba, she does so only by accident.

Galinda

Galinda is a vain Gillikinese girl who becomes Elphaba's roommate at Shiz. Although Galinda is intelligent and shows a real talent for sorcery, her true ambitions are for social and financial security. Elphaba keeps trying to get Glinda (as Galinda comes to be known) to think about the political and social realities of Oz, but Glinda is content merely to flit across the surface, relying on her looks and charm to see her through. As Elphaba and Nessarose become known as the Wicked Witches, Glinda becomes known as the Good Witch. She marries Sir Chuffery. They have no children, and she is stupendously wealthy.

Gawnette

Gawnette is an impoverished resident of Rush Margins who runs a grubby nursery for children. Boq and Elphaba meet in this nursery as children.

Glinda

See Galinda **Grommetik** Madame Morrible's tiktok machine, who serves as her servant, spy, and, in the case of Dr. Dillamond, assassin.

Irji

The eldest son of Fiyero and Sarima, Irji is a soft and dreamy boy who shows a religious bent. He is brutally murdered when the Wizard's forces use the "Paraffin Necklace" on him.

Killyjoy

Killyjoy is Elphaba's beloved dog whom she befriends on the caravan to the Vinkus territory. He becomes the father to a whole pack of wolf like dogs, and he is killed by the Tin Woodman, who mistakes his mission of welcome for an attack.

Liir

Liir is an urchin boy who accompanies Elphaba to Kiamo Ko. Elphaba cannot be sure whether he is the son of her union with Fiyero or not, since she does not remember much of her first two years in the mauntery. Nearly killed by Manek, who locks him in a fishwell, Liir is both fat and slow, and he is a target of teasing by the other children.

Manek

Manek, the second son of Fiyero and Sarima, is bold and cruel. He tells Liir to hide in the fishwell, nearly killing him. He is in turn killed by a falling icicle, which may or may not be Elphaba's doing.

Oatsie Manglehand

Oatsie leads the caravan across the Kumbrica pass to the Vinkus territory and safely delivers Elphaba and Liir to Kiamo Ko.

Milla

Milla is a classmate of Elphaba's from Shiz; she eventually marries Boq.

Madame Morrible

Headmistress of the girls' college at Shiz where Elphaba, Nessarose, and Glinda all attend university, she is an evil woman, who seeks to enchant the three girls in order to bind them to the Wizard's tyrannical purposes. Elphaba tries to kill her the night Fiyero dies, but she fails. After the death of Nessarose, Elphaba sets out to finish the task, but she arrives too late and must settle for bashing in the head of a dead old woman.

Nanny

Originally Melena's nanny, Nanny arrives after Elphaba is born to help with the frightening green child. She is bawdy and honest, and she is the one person to whom everyone speaks the truth. When Melena dies, she raises Elphaba and Nessarose, and she accompanies Nessarose to Shiz. She finds Elphaba at Kiamo Ko and remains with her in old age.

Princess Nastoya

Nastoya is an enchanted Elephant masquerading as the princess of the Scrow people. She reveals herself to Elphaba and advises her on how to survive in difficult times.

Dr. Nikidik

Dr. Nikidik takes over as professor of life sciences after the death of Dr. Dillamond, but he betrays Dr. Dillamond's cause when he shows a willingness to experiment on the Lion cub, Brr.

Nor

Nor, the daughter of Fiyero and Sarima, is a

dreamy child. It is Nor who invites the Wizard's forces into the castle. The lone survivor of the Arjiki royalty, she is kept in chains by the Wizard, and she appears to have lost her mind under his brutal treatment.

Pfannee

Pfannee is a wealthy girl at Shiz who plays a cruel prank on Elphaba and Galinda when she writes a false letter as Galinda, inviting Elphaba to come join them during summer vacation.

Sarima, Dowager Princess of the Arjikis

Sarima is Fiyero's wife, to whom he was betrothed as a child. They have three children together. After leaving the mauntery, Elphaba journeys to Kiamo Ko, the princesses' castle, in order to confess her affair with Fiyero and beg her forgiveness. Sarima, however, refuses to hear Elphaba's confession and refuses to bestow her forgiveness. She is captured and killed by the Wizard's troops while Elphaba is on a visit to Colwen Grounds.

Scarecrow

The Scarecrow is one of Dorothy's companions, whom Elphaba mistakes for Fiyero in disguise. He is also a source of folk superstition among the Munchkinlanders, who make little scarecrow pins and believe in the return of a mythical scarecrow figure.

Shell

Shell is Elphaba's youngest sibling, born during their years in the Quadling country. His birth was the cause of Melena's death, and he grows up to be a secret agent for Munchkinland independence.

Shenshen

Shenshen is one of the cruel wealthy girls at university at Shiz.

Eminent Thropp

Eminent Thropp, Elphaba's great-grandfather, is the head of the Unionist faith in Munchkinland and resides in Colwen Grounds. When he dies, his position is supposed to go to Elphaba, but in her absence Nessarose ascends to the Eminence. After Nessarose dies, Elphaba again refuses to ascend to the Eminence, preferring to leave the Munchkinlanders to rule themselves.

Elphaba Thropp

Also known as the Third Thropp Descending, though she disowns the title, and named Wicked Witch of the West by those who fear her, Elphaba is the protagonist of the novel. Born green, with a mouth full of razor sharp baby teeth, she is an outcast her entire life. She is loved by Fiyero and is probably Liir's mother; she is also, it seems, the biological daughter of the Wizard. Elphaba seeks justice for all creatures. Her lifelong struggle against self-loathing gets the better of her as she sees her hopes and dreams dashed one by one and after she loses her love, Fiyero. She is killed by accident when Dorothy throws a bucket of water on her to douse her skirts, which have caught fire.

Melena Thropp

Elphaba's mother, Melena, is a charismatic, sensual, alcoholic, beautiful woman who marries Frex in order to escape Colwen Grounds. She falls in love with Turtle Heart, and after his death she goes to the Quadling country with Frex as a missionary. She dies giving birth to her third child, Shell. She is loved and mourned by her family.

Nessarose Thropp

Elphaba's younger sister, Nessarose, is born spectacularly beautiful despite not having any arms. An invalid and a religious fanatic, she is needy and self-centered. Frex makes her a pair of exceptionally beautiful shoes, and Glinda enchants them to give Nessarose the balance she has previously lacked so she can finally stand unaided on her own two feet. When Elphaba disappears, Nessarose ascends to the role of Eminent Thropp, and when Munchkinland secedes from Oz, she names herself political leader. Her despotic rule leads her subjects to name her Wicked Witch of the East, and they do not mourn her when Dorothy's house crushes her to death.

Tibbett

Tibbett, with Crope, is one half of a pair of "inverted"—that is, gay—students at the university in Shiz. Tibbett has a traumatic experience in the Philosophy Club from which he really never recovers. Brought into Elphaba's ward of dying patients, he insists on her individuality, and he teases and gossips her back into the world before he dies.

Tin Woodman

See Nick Chopper

Turtle Heart

Turtle Heart is a Quadling glassblower who wanders into Melena's yard one day; the entire family falls in love with him. He stays with them until Nessarose is born. The night of her birth, he is brutally murdered by Munchkinlanders at the behest of the Clock of the Time Dragon. He is probably Nessarose's biological father.

Two, Three, Four, Five, and Six

Sarima's sisters who come to live in Kiamo Ko

are named with numbers reflecting their birth order. They are a gossipy bunch who resent their sister for failing to provide them with husbands. They are brutally murdered by the Wizard's forces.

The Wizard

A human from Earth, the Wizard came to Oz in a hot-air balloon seeking the Grimmerie, a book of magic he had seen in Madame Blavatsky's crystal ball. Once in Oz, he becomes a despot and tyrant, dividing the nation along ethnic lines in order to consolidate power. He escapes Oz in his balloon mere hours before the revolutionaries who seek to kill him. He is probably Elphaba's biological father.

Yackle

By turns an old gypsy woman and an ancient maunt, Yackle is a constant and mysterious presence on the edges of Elphaba's story. The Dwarf tells her that Yackle is the opposite of a guardian angel, that while she has been sent to watch over Elphaba, it may not be for the best. It is Yackle who provides the herbs that might have caused Nessarose's disability, Yackle who comforts Elphaba in the mauntery after Fiyero's death, and Yackle who gives her the broom that she eventually discovers is enchanted.

Themes

Evil

Maguire has stated in a number of interviews that he began writing *Wicked* because he wanted to explore the question of whether a person is born evil or becomes evil over time. Elphaba is certainly born with the fairy-tale indications of evil. She has skin "as green as sin" and a mouth full of razor-sharp teeth—with which her first act after birth is to bite off the finger of one of the crones. Her first word is "horror," and after disappearing she is found in the arms of a demonic animal whose presence is never explained. She certainly seems slated for evil, and yet, as Frex tells her after Nessarose dies, although during those first years she was "a little beast," it was by caring for Nessarose that she became a "normal child." For all her early signs of being "born evil," Elphaba grows up to be a studious, intense, and deeply caring person. Although she rejects the faith in which she was raised, and indeed rejects even the idea that she possesses a soul, Elphaba spends much of her adult life resisting those who perpetrate injustice against others, whether those others be Animals or the poor or the dying she tends in the mauntery wards. She and Fiyero argue over her tactics when she is part of the terrorist underground, for if to do evil is to cause intentional harm to another, then what Elphaba is planning constitutes an evil act. They argue about whether violence against a repressive regime is ever justified. What about the potential for innocent bystanders to become victims of that violence? "What is worse?" Elphaba asks Fiyero during an argument on the topic. "Suppressing the *idea* of personhood or suppressing, through torture and incarceration and starvation, *real living* persons?" It is the thought of these real living persons, oppressed by the Wizard, that eats at Elphaba and that fuels her work. However, for all her talk, when confronted with a swarm of innocent children who surround Madame Morrible, Elphaba finds herself unable to sacrifice them to the cause. She chooses the immediate good of those children over the potential political good of ridding the world of Madame Morrible. After her failed assassination and Fiyero's subsequent death, Elphaba had a choice. She could have hardened her anger and gone further into the underground, becoming even more radicalized, but instead we see that she is brokenhearted and turns to the mauntery, turns back to the missionary work of her childhood, and works out her brokenness in service to others. Again, this is hardly the work of an evil person.

Topics for Further Study

- *The Wizard of Oz* was a children's story published by L. Frank Baum in 1900, as a movie released in 1939, and as *Wicked* in 1995. Starting with the original, write a paper comparing and contrasting these three versions of the story. Pay special attention to issues of audience, historical context, and medium (film versus written word).

- Split the class into groups. Using the *Wicked* soundtrack and information available on Stephen Schwartz's Web site (http://www.musicalschwartz.com/wicke have each group choose an element of the novel that was *not* incorporated into the musical. Write a song, including both lyrics and music, that incorporates that element of the story into the musical. Stage the song, complete with costumes, and make a video of each performance. Have the groups discuss each other's choices of topic, music, lyrics, and performance.

- Maguire used the framework of Baum's novel as a starting point for his own reimagining of the Oz story in three novels. Do the same on a smaller scale. Pick a character and write a first-person monologue (that is, a speech by only one person, who refers to himself or herself as "I") in which your character explains why and how he or she is misunderstood or misrepresented in the novel. Follow your monologue with a short paper analyzing how the story might have turned out differently if this character had only been correctly understood or interpreted by others.

- Elphaba lives in a world in which physiognomy (facial features and appearance) are seen as markers of tribe, ethnicity, and social class. Although her greenness does not mark her as a member of an outcast ethnic or tribal group, the singularity of her skin color does affect both her self-image and her relationships with the people around her. Research the history of physiognomy as it relates to race, class, gender, and theories of human intelligence and character. Prepare a PowerPoint presentation, complete with illustrations, that traces how scientists have interpreted these features in the past and compare them to current views on the subject.

- The geography of Oz is central to many elements of the plot. Workings in teams and using the map in the front of the novel as a starting point, develop a computer game or board game that demonstrates what dangers lie in the various regions of the country and what obstacles must be overcome in order to free the Emerald City from the despotic Wizard. Use as many characters and plot elements from the novel as possible.

- Elphaba is obsessed with the oppression of Animals and is determined to prove Dr. Dillamond's theory that a common thread unites human beings, sentient Animals, and other animals. Although we do not have sentient Animals of the sort that Maguire imagines in the novel, there are many who argue that animals have inherent rights just like human beings do. Research animal rights activist organizations and their arguments. Analyze the premises from which they proceed—what legal rights and moral rights are they claiming for animals? What precedent exists for these claims? Make a multimedia presentation to your class that explains not only the controversy over animal rights but the legal and philosophical underpinnings for those arguments.

Elphaba's long period in the mauntery leaves her changed, though. She is less conscious of her own motives and has lost herself in some crucial way. Her first acts of witchcraft come almost unconsciously: the bees that attack the cook, the icicle that kills Manek; neither of these is consciously willed on Elphaba's part, and yet, could a less damaged person have prevented them? By the time Elphaba journeys to Kiamo Ko, she is a deeply wounded person, incapable of most normal human relations. She does not know whether Liir is her son, although the evidence points that way, and in her wounded state she is incapable of treating him as if he is her son, or unwilling to do so. The trauma of losing Fiyero and of failing in her role as terrorist, seems to have broken some capacity in Elphaba for kindness, empathy, and loving action.

She retreats deeper and deeper into herself and into her projects, often at the expense of those around her. As Elphaba discovers her magical powers, she seems unable to use them to effect any good in the world, and she retreats deeper and deeper into paranoia and agitation. By the end of the novel, she has ironically assumed the title "Wicked Witch of the West," and in doing so she seems to have given herself permission to act accordingly. Although her refusal of power could be seen as modesty, it could just as easily be read as a rejection of a leadership role. Maguire has drawn a portrait of a character who, for most of her life, is a virtuous person and yet allows evil to creep up on her nonetheless.

Aristocracy

Although the Wizard has deposed the Ozma, the hereditary ruler of Oz, the country is still ruled by an aristocracy, that is, a select group of people, chosen by birth, social status, and ethnicity. Elphaba is the rightful heir to the position of Eminent Thropp, complete with religious power and the mansion at Colwen Grounds. Throughout the novel, characters size up one another according to physiognomy, heredity, economic status, ethnicity, and status as Animal or human. The assignment of status according to these largely unearned categories is one of the social injustices against which Elphaba rebels. Although Elphaba inherits the status of the Eminence, her green skin and odd appearance have always made her an outcast. As such, her sympathies lie with the outcasts of society, those who do not have access to the sorts of wealth and power that Galinda aspires to and, as Glinda, achieves. Nessarose, also an outcast because of her disability, takes the opposite tack, using her beauty, invalidism, and religiosity to amass both clerical and secular power. Because Elphaba is so exquisitely aware that the possession of power necessarily means having power *over* someone else, she rejects it at every turn. When Nessarose dies, the Wizard wants to know whether she intends to take over rulership of Munchkinland, and Elphaba's natural reply is that it is time for the Munchkinlanders to rule themselves. Trapped in an aristocratic world, Elphaba rebels against the inherent unfairness of the system.

Destiny

Although Elphaba rejects the religion of her father, the very notion of religion, of God, and the idea that she possesses a soul, she cannot quite shake the idea that she, Glinda, and Nessarose are each at the mercy of a predetermined course of events that they do not entirely understand. Elphaba's birth and her bizarre appearance cause her parents to speculate about what she *means*. Frex tells her on his deathbed, "You were born to curse my life," which implies that

Elphaba exists solely as a lesson to her father. To be seen by all as a signifier of something outside oneself is necessarily to demean one's own humanity and agency (that is, the power to take action), and one of the forces against which Elphaba must continually arm herself is the interpretation of her appearance by others. Even her eventual identity as Wicked Witch of the West is not something she assigns herself but a label that others place onto her. The clothing that she chooses for practicality, humility, and to protect herself from water is read as a witch's costume, and events that Elphaba may or may not have caused are attributed to her. Destiny also appears as a theme when Madame Morrible casts her binding spell on the three girls. Elphaba spends the rest of her life wondering whether it took effect and wondering whether she is the pawn that the Wizard accused her of being when she and Glinda traveled to the Emerald City. Is she the force behind her own life, or is she, as she imagines in her increasing paranoia toward the end of the story, a mere pawn, someone put on earth to act out a predetermined drama? It is a question that Maguire never entirely answers.

Style

Fantasy

Although fantasy novels often use elements of the world as we know it, they are distinguished by the way they create, as Roger Fowler and Peter Childs point out in *The Routledge Dictionary of Literary Terms*, "their own coherently organized worlds and myths." In *Wicked*, the use of fantasy is twofold. First, there is the fantasy world created by L. Frank Baum and imagined on screen by Victor Fleming in the 1939 film. Then there is Maguire's reimagining of those versions, both of which were meant for children, as a serious novel for adults. As such, the novel deals with all the nuances and complications of life that we often try to hide from children: sex, violence, political repression, love, death, and mourning. Elphaba is born green but apparently human, with a mouth full of razor sharp baby teeth, a fantastical occurrence that immediately places us in another world. Her father is a minister in the Unionist faith, a faith that resembles any number of Protestant religions in our world but does not match any of them. In addition, Oz comes with its own coherent mythologies, such as the story of Lurline, the Fairy Queen who founded Oz, and her matrilineal descendents, the Ozmas. There is magic still operating in this world, a magic that can be studied in college the way science or religion can be studied. Finally, there are the Animals, fully sentient animals who speak and reason and function in the world as humans do, despite their animal forms. All of these imaginings mark a world separate from our own, similar enough that we recognize the motivations and desires of its inhabitants and yet distant enough to allow us the freedom to believe that reality can unfold there in ways it cannot unfold here.

Anthropomorphism

L. Frank Baum's use of anthropomorphism, that is, the ascribing of human characteristics to animals, is one of the most commonly cited reasons why some librarians refused, for decades, to stock the Oz books on their shelves. Maguire takes literary device one step further by anthropomorphizing some Animals while others remain devoid of human characteristics. He speculates about what the real consequences would be in a world where animals could think and speak and feel as human beings do. Would we need to accord Animals the same rights as humans? What accommodations would we need to make for their physical differences? When Glinda meets Dr. Dillamond on the train, he asks her to hand his ticket to the conductor, since he has only hooves, not fingers. Anthropomorphized animals are a classic element of fantasy literature, but by taking seriously the consequences of a world shared with sentient animals, Maguire asks readers to think through the political, social, and economic ramifications of anthropomorphism. Maguire imagines Animals existing in a sort of limbo, since they are not considered quite human; they are vulnerable to persecution when the Wizard seeks to divide his people in order to keep a political grip on the realm. In this way, one could also read the fate of the Animals in *Wicked* as analogous to the manner in which African Americans were treated for the first two centuries and more of United States history. Defenders of slavery argued that blacks were subhuman, a separate species, and that they were hardly more than sentient animals. Hence, slave owners argued that the slaves could not take care of themselves and were fit only to serve white masters, who were erroneously perceived to be higher on the Great Chain of Being. Maguire alludes to this historical reality in our world by dramatizing how human beings define difference and use it for political gain, and he uses the literary convention of anthropomorphism to serve the adult ambitions of his novel.

Hero/Antihero

Elphaba is in many ways a typical antihero, that is, a flawed and problematic protagonist. Although she does not lack physical or moral courage, her position as an outsider and her refusal to accept any of the mantles of power that are offered to her mark her as antiheroic. In *Wicked*, Elphaba's antiheroic qualities, her odd color, her physical oddness, her spiky reliance on irony, and her intelligence are all contrasted with the traditional qualities of female heroes displayed by her foils (characters that serve to highlight certain qualities through contrast), Glinda and Nessarose. Whereas Elphaba is considered unattractive, Glinda relies on her physical beauty to get ahead. Where Elphaba dives into her studies and is determined to develop her intelligence as far as possible while at Shiz, Glinda often shies away from her own intelligence, content with a sort of glittery performance of charm to see her through. If Glinda represents the qualities of a traditional female hero (often a princess) of beauty, charm, and conventional goodness, then Elphaba stands next to her as a sort of anti-princess. She is green, ungainly, not charming, and seemingly unconcerned with whether people like her or not. However, her deep concern for true moral goodness and her determination to do the virtuous thing mark her as heroic, although she does not have any of the traditional, external markers of a hero. If Glinda represents one version of female hero, the princess who gets her rich prince in the end, Nessarose represents a different version of the female hero, the religious virgin. Nessarose is also beautiful, despite her handicap. She is the brave invalid who persists in the face of her physical limitations and who turns to religion for solace. Nessarose represents the literary convention of the fierce female virgin, who takes refuge in the public perception of goodness that comes with virginity and religiosity. Maguire makes clear through her actions that these qualities do not necessarily serve Nessarose or her subjects well, that is, she might be religious and virtuous, but that does not save her from becoming a despot whose main ambition is to gain and keep power. Maguire sets up Elphaba as an antihero in order to call into question the traditional qualities of female heroism, and despite Elphaba's fall into wickedness at the novel's end, for most of the story she is the one person who acts in heroic ways, despite her antiheroic appearance.

Historical Context

In an interview for the *Theater Mania* Web site, Maguire told Erika Milvy that when he began writing *Wicked* in the early 1990s, he wanted to "explore, using fictional techniques, the nature and the range of evil—and of how we come to decide who is bad and who is good." Although he originally intended to write about Hitler, he found as he worked that his models for evil came closer to the villains of his young adulthood, particularly Richard Nixon of the Watergate scandal. For someone like Maguire, born in 1956, the political scandals of the 1970s were a loss of political innocence. Learning that President Nixon had overstepped the authority of his office by authorizing unconstitutional wiretaps of his enemies, using the Central Intelligence Agency, the Federal Bureau of Investigation, the Internal Revenue Service, and even the National Security Agency to spy on his political rivals and that he had allowed supporters to break into the headquarters of the Democratic National Committee was enormously shocking, so shocking that it led the president to resign shortly before impeachment hearings were to begin. The United States had always prided itself on being a nation of laws, a nation that respected the separation of powers, and Nixon's violation of those principles was a blow to the country. As Maguire said in the same interview with Milvy, "Nixon and Watergate was the first time I felt politically cynical."

Compare & Contrast

- **1900:** L. Frank Baum publishes *The Wizard of Oz* to immediate critical acclaim and popular success. In 1902, Baum stages the first musical version of the book.

  1995: Maguire reimagines the story of the Wicked Witch of the West and publishes it as *Wicked*, his first adult novel.

  Today: Maguire continues to reimagine Baum's world of Oz, adding two sequels: *Son of a Witch* and *A Lion among Men*. Mean while, the Broadway musical *Wicked* breaks box-office records in cities around the world.

- **1900:** The first wave of the feminist movement is coming to a close as pioneers such as L. Frank Baum's mother-in-law, Matilda Joslyn Gage, and Elizabeth Cady Stanton begin to die. At the turn of the twentieth century, women win the vote only in Colorado and Idaho. It is not until 1920 that the Nineteenth Amendment extends the right to vote to women on a national level.

1995: First Lady Hillary Rodham Clinton travels to Beijing and gives a forceful address to the United Nations World Women's Conference, declaring: "If there is one message that echoes forth from this conference, let it be that human rights are women's rights, and women's rights are human rights, once and for all."

Today: After running for president, Hillary Rodham Clinton loses the nomination to Barack Obama but is appointed as his Secretary of State, continuing her lifelong commitment to the "pursuit of our human rights agenda, not compromising on our principles, but doing what is most likely to make them real."

- **1900:** Although William McKinley wins the presidential election, he is assassinated in September 1901 after serving a mere six months. Theodore Roosevelt becomes the nation's youngest president at age forty-two and institutes a number of Progressive reforms, including railroad regulation, meat and food inspection legislation, and reining in corporate wrongdoing.

1995: While President Clinton ran for president in 1992 on a number of progressive positions, his failure to secure health-care reform combined with his support of the Welfare Reform bill in 1995 loses the support of many progressives in his own party.

Today: Another surge of progressive political optimism accompanies President Barack Obama into office in 2009, when he begins his term by tackling health-care reform.

Although it was Nixon that Maguire was thinking of when he created the Wizard, it was actually the steady erosion of constitutional rights as evidenced in scandals such as the Iran-Contra affair that Maguire saw happening in American politics throughout the 1980s and into the 1990s that inspired him. In the same interview in *Theater-Mania*, Maguire noted: "Everything the Wizard says is wonderful and creepy and it could also be said about Nixon and to some extent, Ronald Reagan."

By the time the musical adaptation debuted in 2003, the creeping despotism of the Wizard's regime began to look to many like an allegory for the erosion of privacy protections that the Bush administration instituted after the terrorist attacks of September 11, 2001, in an effort to prevent future attacks. As Maguire told *Theater-Mania*, "None of us could know when Bush was elected that he would turn out to have such dictatorial tendencies, or that 9/11 was going to stoke up a certain kind of patriotism that would promote a blindness and muteness among citizens and members of Congress … that we would be living under a spell for seven years."

Although Maguire has been outspoken about the specific American politicians upon whom he based the Wizard and his tactics of fear-mongering, stoking ethnic and class divisions, and oppression of minorities, the novel is not a strict political allegory. The Wizard's tactics are representative of a set of techniques common to despots. Along the same lines, although the tactics of Elphaba's revolutionary anarchists are similar to the tactics used during the late 1980s and early 1990s by both political subversives in Latin America and ecological protest groups in the United States, those activities are not an exact allegory either. Although there are historical precedents for some of the characters and their actions, the novel remains a dramatization of how evil affects all parties: the victims, the perpetrators, and those who resist its forces.

Critical Overview

When *Wicked* was published in 1995 it was Maguire's first book for adults. He had made a name for himself in the seventeen years he had been publishing children's books, so the adult themes and content of *Wicked,* as well as his audacious retelling of an American classic, came as something of a surprise to critics used to thinking of him as a children's author. Michiko Kakutani of the *New York Times* was one of Maguire's first real critics, claiming that Maguire's book was "deadly dull." Her central objection seemed to be that where Baum's original was charming because it was pure fantasy, Maguire's "insistence on politicizing Oz and injecting it with a heavy dose of moral relativism turns a wonderfully spontaneous world of fantasy into a lugubrious allegorical realm." Kakutani was in the minority, however, as novelist John Updike, quoted by Stephen Fraser in his interview with Maguire in *Writing!*, called it "an amazing novel," and Robin J. Schwartz in *Entertainment Weekly* said the book was "anything but heavy-handed … thanks to Maguire's impish sense of humor." Robert Rodi, in the *Albany Times Union*, noted that the genius of the book lies in the way that Maguire takes a universally recognizable character and asks the reader to "accept a retrofitted history of how an otherwise well-meaning woman went so wrong."

The novel sold almost two million copies, and

in 2003, it was made into an award-winning Broadway musical. The musical version has played in cities around the world and has brought millions more readers to Maguire's novel.

What Do I Read Next?

- *Son of a Witch* is the sequel to *Wicked*. Released in 2005, this novel follows the story of Liir, the son of Elphaba and Fiyero. Like *Wicked*, this is an adult novel and contains scenes of violence and adult sexuality. It picks up where the first novel left off and continues Maguire's quest to locate the source of evil in society.

- *A Lion among Men* completes the "Wicked Years" trilogy. Published in 2008, this book follows Brr, otherwise known as the Cowardly

Lion, who does indeed turn out to be the same terrified lion club that Dr. Nikidik used in his life sciences experiment in *Wicked*. Brr, searching for information about Elphaba, seeks out the dying maunt, Yackle. As armies close in around the Emerald City, Brr and Yackle spar to obtain crucial information before it is too late. Like Maguire's other two novels in this series, this is a book for adults and contains adult scenes of violence and sexuality.

- *The Wonderful Wizard of Oz* by L. Frank Baum was published in 1900 and is the first in a series of forty books chronicling the history of Oz. Unlike *Wicked, The Wonderful Wizard of Oz* is indeed a story for children. The original illustrations make it clear that Dorothy was, unlike the 1939 movie, quite a young child.

- Maguire cites *The Sword in the Stone* by T. H. White as an example of the kind of book he wanted to write when he started *Wicked*. Originally published in 1938, it is the story of a young boy named Wart who befriends a magician named Merlin. Wart must undergo many trials, including transformation into several animals, and stand up to evil, before it becomes clear that he is the future King Arthur. The first of four books that were eventually published as *The Once and Future King*, this would be suitable for readers too young for the adult themes of the Maguire novels.

- *Animal Rights: Current Debates and New Directions* (2005) is an anthology edited by Cass Sunstein and Martha Nussbaum, two law professors noted for their work on behalf of oppressed peoples. (Nussbaum is also a noted philosopher.) This is an academic anthology that brings together essays by philosophers, activists, and lawyers working on behalf of animal rights. Although not an easy read, it is a balanced introduction to all sides of these difficult issues.

- Alison Lurie writes novels for both adults and children, and she has long been interested in children's literature. In *Boys and Girls Forever: Children's Classics from Cinderella to Harry Potter*, published in 2002, she collects fourteen essays on the enduring appeal of fairy tales and children's literature. For readers interested in the way Maguire used the material of Oz, Lurie's essays should prove illuminating.

- *Daughter of the Flames*, published by Zoe Marriott in 2008, is the story of Zira, the last surviving heir to the Ruan throne. Although her surroundings are some what Middle Eastern, she lives in a fantasy world unique to the novel. Zira must pass through fire in order to regain her title, and she must battle her uncle Abheron, who has usurped her throne. *Daughter of the Flames* is a satisfying young-adult fantasy novel with an interesting multicultural twist.

Sources

Baum, L. Frank, *The Annotated Wizard of Oz*, edited by Michael Patrick Hearn, W. W. Norton, 2000, pp. 89–90.

Boyer, Paul S., *Oxford Companion to American History*, Oxford University Press, 2001, pp. 677, 819.

Childs, Peter, and Roger Fowler, "Fantastic," in *The Routledge Dictionary of Literary Terms*, Routledge, 2006, pp. 82–83.

"Father Knows Best," in *Oprah.com*, ://www.oprah.com/relationships/Incredible-Fathers-and-Their-Families/10 (accessed January 4, 2010).

Fraser, Stephen, "Wicked with Words, Gregory Maguire Reimagines Fairy Tale," in *Writing!* February-March 2006, p. 8.

Goldberg, Bev, "Gregory Maguire's Wicked Beginnings," in *AL Inside Scoop*, July 15, 2009, http://www.alx.ala.org/insidescoop/2009/07/15/grego maguires-wickedbeginnings/ (accessed January 3, 2010).

"Gregory Maguire Brews Another Wicked Mix of Historical Fiction and Timeless Myth," in *Bookselling This Week*, September 16, 2003, http://news.bookweb.org/mbin/printer_friendly? article_id=1800 (accessed January 3, 2010).

Kakutani, Michiko, "Let's Get This Straight, Glinda

Was the Bad One?," in *New York Times*, October 24, 1995, http://www.nytimes.com/1995/10/24/books/books-of-the-times-let-s-get-this-straight-glinda-was-the-badone.html?scp=1&sq=Gregory+Maguire&st=nyt (accessed January 3, 2010).

Landler, Mark, "Clinton Defends Human Rights Approach," in *New York Times*, December 14, 2009, http://www.nytimes.com/2009/12/15/world/15clinto (accessed January 3, 2010).

Maguire, Gregory, *Wicked: The Life and Times of the Wicked Witch of the West*, Harper Collins, 1995.

Milvy, Erika, "A Wicked Writer," in *TheaterMania.com*, February 23, 2009, http://www.theatermania.com/sanfrancisco/news/02-2009/a-wicked-writer_17655.html (accessed January 3, 2010).

Minzesheimer, Bob, "'Wicked' Author Gregory Maguire Casts His Spell," in *USA Today*, October 12, 2005, http://www.usatoday.com/life/books/news/2005-10-12-gregory-maguire-interview_x.htm (accessed January 3, 2010).

Rodi, Robert, "'Wicked' a Marvelous Fantasy Novel of Ideas," in *Albany Times Union*, November 28, 1995, p.D2.

Schwartz, Robin J., "Wicked, The Life and Times of the Wicked Witch of the West," in *Entertainment Weekly*, November 17, 1995, p. 73.

Tyler, Patrick E., "Hillary Clinton, in China, Details Abuse of Women," in *New York Times*, September 6, 1995, http://www.nytimes.com/1995/09/06/world/hillary-clinton-in-china-details-abuse-of-women.html (accessed January 3, 2010).

Further Reading

Auxier, Randall E., and Phil Seng, eds., *The Wizard of Oz and Philosophy*, Open Court, 2008.

> This book is part of a series that examines classics of popular culture from a philosophical point of view. Many of the questions that Maguire addresses in *Wicked* are examined in this collection, including moral theories of virtue and evil.

De Giere, Carol, *Defying Gravity: The Creative Career of Stephen Schwartz from "Godspell" to "Wicked,"* Applause Books, 2008.

> This biography of Stephen Schwartz explores the creative process of this celebrated composer. De Giere reconstructs both Schwartz's hits and his flops. The book includes an appendix of "Creativity Notes" about the creative process.

Hearn, Michael Patrick, ed., *The Wizard of Oz*, Schocken Books, 1987.

> This is a collection of critical essays on L.

Frank Baum's book, the MGM movie, and the historical reception of the original novels.

> Published before Maguire's novel, it

does not contain any references to *Wicked* or to the musical.

Schiebinger, Lorna, *Nature's Body: Gender in the Making of Modern Science*, Rutgers, 2004.

> Elphaba states that after she proves Dr. Dillamond's theory that Animals and humans are fundamentally the same, she wants to extend that work to gender. In this book, Schiebinger traces the manner in which culture influenced the scientists such as Linnaeus, who did the first classification of life forms. She then goes on to trace how racism and sexism affected the so-called scientific classification of beings and how that in turn affects current scientific exploration.

Singer, Peter, *In Defense of Animals: The Second Wave*, Wiley Blackwell, 2005.

> Peter Singer is a professor of bioethics at Princeton University. His work on the nature of moral thinking, based on utilitarianism, led him in 1975 to write one of the first books on animal rights, *Animal Liberation*. *In Defense of Animals: The Second Wave* continues his thinking on this subject, while taking into account the significant work that has been done by others concerned

with animal consciousness and animal rights since that time.

Suggested Search Terms

Gregory Maguire

Gregory Maguire AND Wicked

Gregory Maguire AND interview

Wicked AND novel

Stephen Schwartz AND Wicked

L. Frank Baum

L. Frank Baum AND Oz

Wicked Witch of the West AND Maguire

Maguire AND Baum

Gregory Maguire AND evil

Gregory Maguire AND fantasy AND Wicked